Light and Counterlight

Also by Mark Miller

Conversing With Stones (Five Islands Press, 1989)
This Winter Beach (Seaview Press, 1999)
Scanning the Horizon (Ginninderra Press, 2018)

Mark Miller

Light and Counterlight

Light and Counterlight
ISBN 978 1 76109 044 8

Cover: *Autumn Valley*, watercolour by Ron C. Moss

First published 2020 by
GINNINDERRA PRESS
PO Box 3461 Port Adelaide 5015 Australia
www.ginninderrapress.com.au

Contents

all the weight of dawn

breaking light
the pale vibrato
of cherry blossoms

bent grass stem
all the weight of dawn
in the dewdrop

water beads
stretching leaf to leaf
spider's silk

Ngunnawal dawn
out of the ashes the nutty paste
of Bogong moths

sunlit snow
the radiant throat
of a honeyeater

spring rain
a butcherbird pipes up and down
its woodwind scales

snowmelt
the scent of pine needles
with each step

reed notes rising from the rushes a pied butcherbird

clear mountain summit
drinking from the same tarn
day moon and I

out of the silence

sudden breeze
every strand of the spider's web
in tune

creek's green algae
a water-strider sucks
on a fly

parting grass a snake slips out of the silence

wedge-tailed eagles
the farmer counts
his lambs

forest trail
a torn owlet's wing
slick with spittle

spring shower
magpies taste
and sing the rain

skittering kite-tail across the sky a child's laughter

sunlight through cherry blossoms a girl glides in her wheelchair

night currents

whispering brook
so many secrets
lost to the sea

moon rising over the lake frog chorus

deepening dusk
harbour yachts moored
to the silence

neap tide flipping onto its back a caught fish

night currents
moving beneath the surface
jellyfish moon

closed roadside stall
a barn owl eyes
the honesty box

sultry night
the neighbour's cat
begins its caterwaul

on dry sand

daylight breaking
origami of a white egret
takes flight

harbour dawn
the ship's horn opening
a space in mist

ebb tide
only the querulous cries
of oystercatchers

estuarine mudflat
the dot art busyness
of soldier crabs

on dry sand
the old boatshed
leans on its shadow

scaling his catch
hands of the old fisher
sequined with light

wind-blown dune
a green shoot through
a dead cormorant's wing

in the jellyfish tide a bloated plastic bag

cracked claypan
tourists take selfies
in the shell middens

across spinifex

heatwave
the horizon's haze
of locust nymphs

across spinifex
the running flame
of a fox

fire ban
overhead a goshawk fans
the thermal currents

gum tree bark
the Dreamtime art
of scribbly moths

forked hay sheaf
coiling out of itself
a brown snake

approaching midday
a lone pine slowly
drinks its shadow

saltbush haze
the rolling dust storm
of a road train

midday heat
the old collie
laps the shade

new estate
I linger where the tree's shadow
used to fall

along the red dirt road

ongoing drought
the stillness
of the rope swing

lorikeets
rainbow fish flipping
in a blue bowl

deep summer
the crack of walnuts
on the outhouse roof

another drought year
along the red dirt road
another hearse

rendezvous
sharing a ripe mango
lips to lips

hollow sound
of the rainwater tank
summer's end

thunder
the scattered pinking
of grass parrots

ping of hail
timpani of unshelled peas
into a bowl

breaking drought
from cupped hands the child
tastes the rain

sun shower
darting this way and that
skink on the cobblestones

on electricity wires
trapeze artists dangling
galahs tipsy with rain

the other side of mist

eventide
on the other side of mist
a dingo's howl

back road at dusk
seeing a kangaroo
in every shadow

summer storm
the brimming moon
in the rain bucket

clearing shower
night rolls out
its trestle of stars

freight train running through the valley the Milky Way

midnight
a lone ferry fills the harbour
with Christmas lights

wild mushrooms

twilight dawn
the night heron
punctures the moon

spider's web anchored at five points the morning star

high tide
the bay's backwash
of diesel spume

parting fog
branches of the plum tree
fruited with finches

wild mushrooms
easily enough for two
in the widow's basket

autumn rain

home from the clinic
shadow on her face
shadow on the film

stepping from the cab
at the hospital gates
autumn rain

emergency room
the tick tick
of the ceiling fan

diagnosis
through the pane starlings
in the bare trees

giving shape to the wind

lipping the fallen eucalyptus leaf the old carp

open heath giving shape to the wind gnarled pencil pine

skeletal leaf
giving back all
that it has taken

scrabbling pigeons
a breastfeeding mum
in the soup queue

melancholic strains
of the busker's fiddle
I miss my train

trees filling with crows

urban hostel
across the hall the strains
of a cowboy song

dusk coming on the trees filling with crows

slow night
the waitress polishes
her nails

cold lakeside
only the sweeping bills
of avocets

skeletal tree
darkness darker now the owl
takes flight

on the face of it moon in the rain bucket

winter pruning

paling sky
birdsong unravels colour
in the yard's bare trees

out of the fog the silence of fence posts

midwinter forest
on milkweed the sighing
of a monarch's wings

pedalling in mist
the road neither before
nor after

stiffness in my fingers winter pruning

first death
my son cradling
our old dog's head

out of the mist
the curving neck
of a black swan

inside the ocean the names of all the rivers

salted wind
all the plastics the tide
gives us back

contrails

foreclosure
hidden by the brim of his hat
the farmer's eyes

auctioneer's spiel
the farm widow's
furrowed brow

contrails
the fading memories
of old adventures

storm clouds darken
the scattered homecoming
of carrion kites

snow
deeper into winter
our footprints

alpine hut
the nightlong hum
of wind in the pines

back from the hospice
on the line her old nightdress
lifts its empty sleeves

cleaning out the drawers
the scent of her perfume
on too many things

the empty swing

art gallery
buttoning up my jacket
before a winter canvas

cave walls
the lost tongues
of ochre figures

talk of war
I nick my finger
with the secateurs

grey dusk falling
a woman in the window opposite
unpins her hair

shadows lengthen
still creaking in the park
the empty swing

power outage
the distant sound
of a saxophone

raven in the withered tree the winter moon

fog settling on the town hall steps a homeless man

into silence

moonless night
yellow light from the window
of my ex-wife's house

night train
the low tones of a stranger's
recent divorce

heavy fog
this dwelling on things
we can't change

flake of grey bark lifting from the branch an owlet nightjar

winter's night
in the finished scarf
a dropped stitch

past midnight
a truck changes down gears
into silence

Acknowledgements

Haiku in this book have previously appeared in the following newspapers, journals and anthologies. My thanks to each of the editors who kindly considered and published my work:

Akitsu Quarterly, Acorn, A Hundred Gourds, Australian Love Poems (ed. Mark Tredinnick, Inkerman & Blunt, 2013), *Award Winning Australian Writing 2017* (Melbourne Books, 2017), *bottle rockets, brass bell: a haiku journal, Butterfly Dream Anthology* (NeverEnding Story, 2018), *cattails, Chrysanthemum, dust devils: The Red Moon Anthology of English-Language Haiku 2016* (ed. Jim Kacian, Red Moon Press, 2017), *Creatrix, Echidna Tracks, Eureka Street, European Haiku Prize Distinguished Poets Anthology 2016, Evening Breeze: Janice M. Bostok Award Anthology* (Australia, 2012), *Failed Haiku, Frameless Sky, FreeXpresSion, Frogpond, ginyu International Haiku Magazine, Guide to Sydney Rivers* (ed. Les Wicks, Meuse Press, 2015), *Haiku Quarterly, Hedgerow, 3Lights, kokako, Mainichi Daily News, Notes From the Gean, paper wasp, Presence, Prospect, Scope* (FAWQ), *Shamrock, still heading out: Australia-New Zealand Haiku Anthology* (paper wasp, 2013), *The Haiku Calendar 2017* (Snapshot Press), *The Heron's Nest, The Vancouver Cherry Blossom Haiku Invitational, tinywords, Under the Basho, Wales Haiku, Wild Plum: Behind the Tree Line Anthology 2015, Windfall: Australian Haiku* (Blue Giraffe Press) and *Yamadera Basho Memorial Museum Haiku Contest Anthology* (2014, 2015, 2016 and 2019)

Awards

'parrots' was awarded an Honourable Mention in the Haiku Quarterly Contest 1989;
'moonless night' was awarded Third Prize in the Mainichi Daily News (Japan) Annual Selection 2008;
'shadows lengthen' was awarded Third Prize in the 12th International Kusamakura Haiku Competition (Japan) 2008;
'night train' was awarded an Honourable Mention in the 13th Mainichi Haiku Contest 2009;
'another drought year' was a finalist and received an Honourable Mention in the Janice M. Bostok Award 2012;
'thinning mist' received an Honourable Mention in the Janice M. Bostok Award 2012;
'breaking light' won an International Sakura Award in the Vancouver Cherry Blossom Festival Haiku Invitational 2013;
'thunder' was awarded first place in the Blue Giraffe Press 2nd Haiku Competition 2014;
'rendezvous' received a European Haiku Distinguished Poets award 2016;
'deepening dusk' was awarded first prize in the FAWQ Haiku Competition 2016;
'winter's night' was runner-up in the Snapshot Press Haiku Calendar Competition 2016; and shortlisted for the H. Gene Murtha Memorial Senryu Contest 2017; and
'on electricity wires', 'parting fog' and 'past midnight' were three parts of a haiku sequence, 'Occasions of Birds', which won the 2018 Henry Lawson Festival Open Poetry Award.

About the Author

Mark Miller is an award-winning poet who has published over 300 haiku in international journals and anthologies, including *Akitsu Quarterly, Acorn, The Red Moon Anthology of English-Language Haiku* 2016, *Janice M. Bostok Award Anthology* 2012, *Frogpond, Presence, Shamrock, The Heron's Nest, Under the Basho* and *Windfall: Australian Haiku.* Among his awards are an International Sakura Award in the Vancouver Cherry Blossom Festival Haiku Invitational 2013, first place in the Blue Giraffe Press Haiku Competition 2014 and first prize in the FAWQ Haiku Competition 2016. His haiku have been translated into languages other than English, including German, Italian, Japanese and Russian. *Light and Counterlight* is Mark's first book of haiku. He lives on the south coast of New South Wales, Australia.

www.ingramcontent.com/pod-product-compliance
Lightning Source LLC
Chambersburg PA
CBHW062143100526
44589CB00014B/1673

* 9 7 8 1 7 6 1 0 9 0 4 4 8 *